The best of
Barcelona

KT-223-462

EDITOR
Ediciones A. CAMPAÑÁ
Alcalde de Móstoles, 26-28 08025 BARCELONA
Tel.: 93 456 43 36 - Fax: 93 450 18 89
e-mail:edicampanya@telefonica.net

FOTOGRAFÍAS
Antoni Campañá Capella

DIRECCIÓN DE PUBLICACIÓN
Margarita Campañá Capella

IMPRESIÓN
FUTURGRÀFIC (Molins de Rei)

FOTOMECÁNICA
JEBA S.L.L. Lepanto 264, 3º-B Barcelona

ISBN: 978-84-86294-45-8   Dep. Legal: B-17.525

Prohibida la reproducción total o parcial de fotografías o textos de este libro.

Barcelona's nomination as the seat of the 1992 Olympic Games changed, once again, the evolution of the city. This historical milestone provided Barcelona with a transformation, the latest among many throughout this city's history.

In this way Barcelona underwent a deep urbanistic change, only comparable to those made for the celebration of the World Exhibitions in 1929 and 1988. Barcelona has recovered a vitality which was lost during the political transition(1975-1985).The Games have definitely given Barcelona, in the phase of eternal development, a magnificent excuse to "finish" the city.

The present Barcelona is a city open to the sea, returning it to its Phoenecian origens, the first traders to reach the Catalan coast and found a centre of business conections with the rest of the Peninsula.

HISTORIC BACKGROUND.

The origins of Barcelona are somewhat confused, plagued even with legends. It is true that the Phoenicians were the first "invaders" and the majority of historians agree that it was the Cartaginese who baptised the city. It was, in fact, Hannibal who, in memory of his father *Amilcar Barca*, gave it the name of Barcino.

The references detected in the archeological remains found at the foot of Montjuic, show, however, that prior to the various invasions and cultures established in Barcelona, there existed a native population whose antiquity is difficult to determine. It does however, fit in perfectly with the other civilizations on the Paleolitic Mediterranean coast.

The Roman domination, which lasted for six centuries, developed the colony "*Julia Augusta Faventia Paterna Barcino*" within the limits of what, in those times, were the natural limits of Barcelona, between the sea and the mountain and between the rivers Besos and LLobregat.

The later invasions of the "*Barberos*" meant the fortification of the city within walls, but the decline of the Roman empire gave place to the Visigoth domination.

From here began the Barcelona's era of greatest expansion and splendour. A fertile trade route with Genova and Venice was established and later the marriage between *Ramon Berenger IV* with the Princess *Petronilla of Aragon* created a vast and rich kingdom. The expansion reached its zenith with the conquests of King *Jaume I*, who drove the Sarracens out of the Balear islands and extended his dominion to *Corsica*, *Sardina* and *Sicily*. In his "crusade" he even

General view of Barcelona.

The king *Ataulfo* established his dominion over the city.

Later, in 716, Barcelona fell into the hands of the Arabs and remained so until 801 when it was freed by *Luis el Piadoso*, the son of Charlemagne. The independance of Barcelona was born from the fight against the Arabs.

The strength and tenacity of the brave Guifre el Pilos, in the fight against Islam, won the heart of *Charlemagne*, who gave the city its independence, a fact which made *Guifre el Pilós* hero of the moment and later a Catalan National Hero.

fought against the Arabs in Greece and Turkey.

In this way Barcelona was converted into the most prosperous city in the Mediterranean and Peninsula, it was the city's era of maximum splendour.

Evidence of this splendour was the large number of stately buildings and walls which were built in this era in what now forms the present nucleus of the city.

A splendour which culminated with the great adventure of the discovery of America. A large number of the ships of the discovery were constructed in the "*Les Drassanes*", the shipyards of Barcelona. Slowly the central government turned its attention to other

The remains of Barcelona's old wall.

The new buildings in Parc de Mar.

parts of the Peninsula. This provoked a rebellion which finished with the confrontation of the Borbonic troops against the city of Barcelona. The city was forced to surrender and lost the privileges of Catalonia, on the 11th September, 1714.

The national rights of Catalonia, the *Consell de Cent* and the *Generalitat* were abolished and the Catalan language was prohibited. As a reprisal against the break imposed by these forces the people of Catalonia declared this day, 11th September, the *"Diada"*, the National festival of Catalonia.

The losses were great for Barcelona and were not limited to the abolition of political rights. More than a thousand buildings were torn down to construct a military fort called *"La Ciutadella"* The demolition of this fort to construct a great park which housed large buildings destined to be museums, according to the plans of *Ildelfons Cerdà* and the celebration of the Universal Exhibition in 1888 gave the people of Barcelona reason to celebrate as they saw the bastion of their dominators destroyed.

It was precisely the *"Plan Cerdà"* begun for this

Exhibition and finished in 1929, which gave Barcelona the possibility to regain its urban strength and citizenship This had begun to recover in the reign of Carlos III, during its phase of imperialistic decline which stressed the need to recover the strong commercial push of the Catalans.

Without a doubt, the final development of the "*Plan Cerdà*" allowed the city to expand into what is now known as "*L'Eixample*". This connects the old quarter to the villages of *Gracia, Les Corts, Sant Gervasi* and *Sarrià*, forming the city as it is known today. The latest remodeling, for the 1992 *Olympic Games* has fashioned the definitive Barcelona, reflecting a new era of commercial expansion, both cultural and political, in accordance with this city's role within the Iberic Peninsula and the cultural framework of the Mediterranean.

Plaça Catalunya with
the staue "La Deesa" (The Godess)
by Josep Clarà.

THE OLD QUARTER.

This is the area within the antique walls and presently bordered by *Les Rondes* which circle the oldest part of Barcelona, inluding the *Barri Gotic*.

To the North is *Plaça Catalunya*, which is the centre of connection with this part and the *L'Eixample*. The Plaça is one of the city's important centres and one of the streets which begins there, *Les Rambles*, which joins it to the sea in a beautiful and picturesque walk, is a delightful part of this city. The innumerable stands which sell birds of all kinds and the marvel of the *Rambla de les Flors*, full of colour and perfume, make up a frame of unequaled beauty and cordial atmosphere. The newspaper stands, authentic open air book shops, for the enjoyment of passersby and, an essential element, the continuous coming and going of all classes of people from all over the world.

Night view of Plaça Catalunya.

Plaça de Catalunya, monument to Francesc Macià.

AROUND THE RAMBLES.

People who may be in a hurry to get somewhere or may just be taking a walk, all of them give the impression of being happy and optimistic just by "*ramblejar*" walking in the *Rambles* of Barcelona.

Begining our walk in the *Plaça Catalunya* down *Les Rambles* towards the sea. First, on the right hand, we come to the *Font de Canaletas*. The legend says that "whosoever drinks from the fountain of Caneletas will always live in Barcelona".

Further down, the first important building is the *Academia de les Ciéncies* and later we find the Baroque style church of *Betlem*, constructed between 1681 and 1729,

Opposite this is *Palau Moya*, better known as *Palau de Comillas*, built in 1771 by *Cayetano Luis de Copóns*. General *Duchenesne* who ordered the trees of the *Rambles* to be planted, lived here during the Napoleonic occupation.

Just where the *Ramble de les Flors* begins we find the *Palau de la Virreina*, begun in 1772 and finished in 1784. Its promoter was *Felip Manuel Amat i Junyent*, viceroy of Peru for more than fifteen years. At present this palace is used for different artistic activities,exhibitions of paintings, photographs, sculpture and others, and is the home of the Decorative Arts Museum.

At the end of the *Ramble de les Flors*, is the *Gran Teatre del Liceu*. This magnificent theatre, finished for the first time in 1848 a project of *Miquel Garriga i Roca*, was destroyed by a fire and rebuilt in 1862 this time under the instructions of *Oriol Mestres* and decorated with paintings by *Martí Alsina, Mestres, Casas* and *Tigalt*. During many years this

The fountain in Portaferrissa.

Canaletes fountain.

A flower stand in Les Rambles.

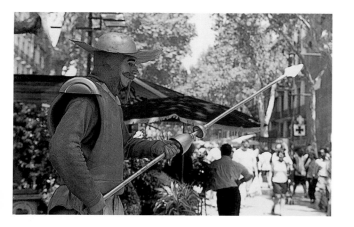

Mosaic by Joan Miró in Plà de la Boquería.

A flower stand in Les Rambles.

theatre has been a symbol of Barcelona's musical tradition and some of the most famous Opera singers in the World have stood upon its stage.

We must move away from the Ramblas a little to see the *Hospital de la Santa Creu* which is at present used by public institutions such as the *Escola Massana d' Arts*, *Biblioteca de Catalunya* and *Conservatori Municipal d' Arts Suntuaries*. Inside may be seen almost three hundred incunabula and more than two thousand manuscripts of great histroric and literary value.

Continuing along *Sant Pau* street, we come to the Romanic church of *Sant Pau del Camp*, built at the beginning of the XII century, in the form of a Greek cross, with barrel vault and dome from the same period. The *XII century* cloisters are admirable and the XIV century rectoral house, originally the old chapter house.

On the other side of the *Rambles* we find one of Barcelona's most beautiful squares. The *Plaça Reial* in Neoclassic style, work of the architect *Daniel Molina*. The square surrounded by porticos, is a harmonic

Flowers are the protagonists in Les Rambles.

reminder of the romantic era. A central fountain is surrounded by elegant street lamps designed by the genius, *Gaudí.*

Just in front of the *Plaça Reial* in *Conde de Asalto* street, we find a splendid example of the work of the architect *Gaudí*, the *Palau del Compte de Güell*, one of the most fantastic creations by this famous Catalan architect. At present it is the *Museu Historic del Teatre.*

Continuing down the Rambles we come to the *Plaça del Teatre* with a monument dedicated to *Frederic Soler*, better known as *Serafí Pitarra*, a great promoter of Catalan theatre. Several of his famous literary works are conserved.

A little further down we find the *Palau Marc*, built in 1776, for a distinguished old family from Reus, this palace has recently been remodeled.

Palau de la Virreina.

La Boquería market.

Casa Bruno Quadros by Josep Vilaseca in Plà de la Boquería.

Casa Figueras, a typical shop in Les Rambles.

The neoclasic style, Plaça Reial.

Plaça Reial,
streetlamps
designed by Gaudí.

Facade of the Gran
Teatre del Liceu.

Night view of Columbus and Porta de la Pau.

The port and Columbus' monument.

A PORT OPEN TO THE SEA.

At the end of the *Rambles* facing the sea is the large square called Porta de la Pau with the *Monument to Columbus*, a modern symbol of Barcelona, in its centre. It was built according to a project by *Cayetano Buigas* and was opened in July 1888. It is 59 metres high and the statue of the sailor measures 7.60 metres. Inside the column there is a lift to the top of the monument where we have a marvellous panoramic view of the city.

The *Portal de la Pau* receives its name from a boat of the same name constructed in 1849 in memory of the peace after the *Matiners war*. This coincided with the moment of Barcelona port's greatest expansion, directed by the Greek *Estagis* and the Barcelonese *Josep Rafo*.

Parallel to the sea and crossing this wide square is the modern and busy, motorway known as *Ronda Litoral*. It goes underground leaving a wide promenade for the people of Barcelona, the *Moll de la Fusta* on the surface. Here we find several restaurants and cafes, with wide sunny terraces and a splendid view of the Port. This area has recently been remodelled and fits in perfectly with *Les Rambles*, the new beaches and the *Vil.la Olimpica*.

On the other side there is one of the best conserved historic buildings in the city, *Les Drassanes*. It is the only building of its period and kind in the world. The Naval Shipyards ordered to be built by King *Jaume I* "*The Conquerer*" in 1208 and later added to by *Pere II* due to Barcelona's maritime traffic are in a marvellous

Porta de la Pau and Les Rambles in the background.

Maritima station, Porta de la Pau and the city in the background.

state of conservation. The building, as it still stands, was finished in 1387 on the orders of *Pere III* and thirty galleys could be built there simultaneously.

Now *Les Drassanes* is used as the *Maritime Museum* and several offices of the *Generalitat*. Diverse popular cultural acts and exhibitions are held here.

Behind *Les Drassanes* part of the wall of Barcelona is conserved, dated from the XV Century. We can see the only remaining gateway, the *Porta de Santa Madrona*, which in some way finishes our walk down the *Rambles* from *Plaça Catalunya*, to the sea passing through some of the most exceptional streets in this city.

THE GOTHIC QUARTER.

Of the many beautiful places in Barcelona, a great part are to be found in the *Barri Gotic*. We can see authentic jewels of Romanic and Gothic styles, dispersed among large buildings of later construction but no less beautiful.

We can go there through the Gothic style church of *Santa Anna* continuing through *Vil.la de Madrid* with the remains of the *II Century Roman Cementry*. Closer to the heart of the old Barcino, is the *Basílica del Pi*, with its bare Catalan Gothic exterior, a bell tower 54 metres high, and its rose window surpassed only by that of the Notre Dame in Paris.

We reach *Plaça Nova* along *Palla* street which brings us to the *Barri Gotic*, the area called *Mons Taber* in medieval texts. Two Roman towers guard the entrance to the walled area, the city's only defense from the II to the XIII centuries. Here, in strong contrast, we find the modern *Architects college*, with friezes referring to Catalan folklore drawn by *Picasso*.

To the right of the Roman towers is the *Episcopal Palace* with a Baroque facade built in the XIII century over the walls. To the left is the *Archdecon's house*, nowadays the *Arxiu Historic de la Cuitat*, built to the orders of the archdeacon *Lluis Desplà* in the XI century and finished in the XV century.

Beside this is the Chapel of *Santa Llucia*, the remains of the Romanic Cathedral built between 1273 and 1275. The present *Cathedral of Barcelona* is the third to be build throughout history.

The first already existed in the year 559 and was destroyed by *Almanzor* in 985, nothing is left. The construction of the second one began in 1046 and was finished and consecrated in 1058. The Romanic remains can still be seen in the present Cathedral, work on which was begun in 1298 but interrupted in 1422.

Of the later additions and reforms, the main facade is worth mention, based on a project by the Frenchman *Mestre Carlí* (1408) it was begun in 1887. The

Night view of Maremagnum.

Cathedral has one of the most beautiful Gothic cloisters in existence. It is Quadrangular, surrounded by chapels on three sides, some of which retain the original XIV and XV century wrought iron grills. The cloister leads on to the *Sala Capitular* built between 1405 and 1454, nowadays it is the *Cathedral Museum*. In the centre of the cloister there is a small temple with a fountain which has become famous for being the scene of "*l'ou con balla*" every year, during *Corpus*. In the interior of the cloister we can see the "geese on the pond" which according to saying symbolize the virgin purity of *Santa Eularia*, co-patron of Barcelona to whom the crypt of the Cathedral is dedicated. The door which leads to *Bisbe* street is called *Santa Eularia*, and dates from the XV Century, the work of *Antoni Claperós* beautifully ornate and shaped.

Passeig de Colón with the staue of the navigator. Montjuïc in the background.

Barcelona Museum of Contemporary Art: MACBA.

Les Drassanes (Royal Shipyards).

Night view of Moll de la Fusta with Columbus in the Background, fron a terrace.

The XV century Santa Madrona gateway in the city walls.

The Gothic
Church,
Colegiata of
Santa Anna.

On entering the *Cathedral* one is struck by the central vault made up of three, beautifully simple, vaulted naves. There are three lateral chapels among the three butresses, the apse is bounded by an aisle with another nine chapels.

Below the central nave is the crypt of *Santa Eularia*, a project by *Jaume Fabre*, an excellent example of Catalan Gothic. Since 1339 this crypt has contained the marble sarcophagous of *Santa Eualria*, an invaluable object sculpted by *Nicolás Pissano*. Beside the high altar we can see the sepulcres of the Catalan monarch *Ramón Berenguer* and his wife *Almodis*, promoters of the XI century cathedral of Barcelona. The choir stalls contain works sculpted by Jordi Johan and the seats by the German *Lochner*. The coats-of-arms on the seats are those of the knights who attended the *Capitulo del Toison de Oro*, held in 1519. The head of a Turk, in remembrance of *Ali Babá*, decapitated in the *Batalla de Lepanto*, hangs from the monumental organ.

Basílica del Pí, with the impressive rose window.

Santa Eularia Cathedral, from Plaça Nova.

Aerial view of the Cathedral and Gothic quarter.

Behind the Catedral in *Comptes* street, we find the building containing the *Arxiu del la Corona d'Aragó* and the Casa de la Inquisició. Further on we find the remains of Visigothic houses and a temple, the *Museu Marés* and in *Baixada de Canonja* street we find the house of *Pia Almoina*, one of the best conserved and oldest monuments in the Gothic quarter. Behind the aspe of the Catherdral, the XIV century *house of the Canonjes* is well worth looking at. Further on in Paradís streeet we find a formidable medie-

Barcelona Cathedral fron Plaça Nova.

val building, belonging to the "*Centre Excursionista de Catalunya*", the oldest sports and cultural centre in Catalonia. Inside this building the columns of the Augusto Temple are conserved, built by the Romans on the highest part of the city. This point is marked by the mill wheel fixed to the floor in *Paradís* street, in front of the above mentioned society, in other words on the summit of *Mons Taber*.

From behind the Cathedral along *Santa Clara* street we reach the *Plaça del Rei*, a marvel of Gothic art

The apse of the Cathedral from Bisbe street.

View of the Gothic quarter from Plaça del comte Ramón Berenguer I, "El Gran".

The Cathedral cloisters and "the geese" of Santa Eularia.

and the scene of events in the history of Barcelona. Despite what is said, however, there is no documentary evidence that it was in this square where the "*Reyes Catolicos*", *Fernando* and *Isabel*, received admiral *Christopher Columbus* on the return from his first voyage to the *Americas*, 3rd April 1493.

Near this square is the *Axiu de la Corona d'Aragó*, built in 1549, directed by *Antoni Carbonell*. The documents guarded in this building are priceless, belonging to the old *Catalano-Aragonese* crown.

Opposite is *Padellàs* house, built in the XVI century at present the *Museu d' Historia de la Ciutat*. The pre-Christian remains of the city can be seen in the cellars.

Next to this is the Capella de *Santa Agueda*, built to the orders of the *King Jaume II* and his wife *Blanca de Anjou* in 1302.

This chapel forms part of the *Main Royal Palace*, built in a Romanic style and finished in the *XIV Century*. The great hall is the *Saló de Tinell*, 35 metres long, 18 wide and 12 high, where a variety of artistic and cultural exhibitions are held.

Above this palace is the *Mirador of King Martí*, a singular, six storied, look-out tower with porticoed galleries,

Cathedral bell tower or "Torre de les Hores".

The equestrian statue of Ramon Berenguer I.

Bisbe street, which connects
the Cathedral to Plaça Sant
Jaume.

which gives character to the *Plaça del Rei*. On arriving at the *Plaça San Jaume*, we find, on the right the *Palace of the Generalitat de Catalunya*. seat of the present Catalan government.

The Renaissance facade is the work of *Pere Blay*, dated 1596 and was added to the rest of the building. The Gothic facade in Bisbe street is much more important, dated from 1416 the work of the architect *Marc Çafont* and the scultor *Pere Johan*,author of the medallion with the image of *Saint George*. This street is crossed by a beautiful bridge which joins the Palau de la Generalitat to the houses on the other side of

the street, the official residence of the *President of the Generalitat de Catalunya*. It was built in 1927 by *Joan Rubio*, and is a summary of Gothic style.

Inside the Generalitat the first thing we see is the original *Pati Gotic*, the prototype of the stately patios in Catalonia. It was built in 1425, by *Marc Çafont*, author of the *Chapel of Saint George* in the interior of the Palace and dated from 1432. A few metres further on is the *Pati dels Taronjers*, built between 1526 and 1600, in its centre we find a *statue of Saint George*, the patron saint of Catalonia, attributed to *Benvenuto Cellini*. The centre of the building is occupied by the

Plaça del Rei and the unusual tower of King Marti.

Hall of Saint George, also built by Pere Blay in 1596.

Opposite this building, we find the *Town Hall* or the *Cases Consistorials*, also known as the *Casa de la Ciutat.* The neoclassic style facade was also added to the old building between 1832-1836.

Inside the Town Hall and after going under the antique Gothic style portal built at the end of the XIV century, we enter such important halls as *Saló de Cent*, which the council of one hundred judges of the city ordered to be built in the second half of the XIV century. This is the place where the hundred *counsellors* deliberated, the antique parliament, whose executive power came from the constituents of the "*Trentenari Antic i Nou*". This hall was begun in 1369 and the first session was held 17th August, 1373.

Next to the *Saló de Cent,* is a small semicircle called *Saló de Sessiones de Reina Regent.* This name is due to a portrait of the *Queen Maria Cristina* with *Alfonso XII*, who presided over it. It was built in 1860.

In the Neoclassic part of the building we find several halls such as the *Alcaldía*, the *Central* or *de Carlos II*, *Consulat de Mar*, or *Saló de Croniques* a sumptuous apartment built in 1929 and decorated by the original artist *Josep Maria Sert*, whose singular paintings

The main facade of the Palau de la Generalitat de Catalunya.

El Pati dels Taronjers, en la Generalitat.

represent some scenes of the Catalans in Oriente under *Roger de Flor*.

We come to the *Via Laietana* along *Llibreteria* street until we come to the *Plaça de Berenguer el Gran*, with its equestrian statue of the King and from where we can see the other facade of the chapel of *Santa Agueda*, the tower, *Mirador del Rei Martí* and the Cathedral Bell Tower, also called *Torre de les Hores de la Cuitat*. Continuing up this street we come to another part of the antique area where we find the *Palau de la Música Catalana*, home of the *Orfeó Català*, where the majority of individual and symphonic music concerts are held. It is the work of the architect *Domenech i Montaner*. When it was first built it was highly controversial, however at present, it is classed as an exceptional piece of work representative of this school which was a landmark in the architectural development of Barcelona. In the centre of the ceiling above the stalls there is a beautiful coloured lamp said to be made by *Gaudí*. This adorns the theatre which is, at present, an authentic symbol of Barcelona and its musical vocation.

Returning to the *Via Laietana* we go along *Princesa*

Barcelona Townhall or Cases Consistorials.

Saló de Cent, in the Townhall.

street, to another beautiful area of the old quarter, *Montcada* street, which begins at the chapel of *Marcus*, built in 1116.

The origin of this street dates from 1153, when Guillém *Ramón de Montcada* obtained permision to build his house in what was then the *Via Nova*. Soon after, other palaces were built forming the most stately street in Barcelona between the XII and XVI centuries. Some of the palaces such as that of the *Marqués de Lió*, *Palau Dalmases* or that of *Baró de Castellet*, are true jewels of architecture.

One of these palaces, the *Palau Berenguer de Aguilar, XIII century*, houses one of the most well known museums in Europe and without a doubt that of widest artist scope in the city. This is the *Museu Picasso* initially created from the donation of an important collection of *Picasso's works* by *Jaume Sabartés*, an intimate friend of this artistic genius. Later, thanks to an important personal donation by the artist himself, of more than 200 oil paintings and thousands of sketches, notes, finished drawings, water colours, pastels and engravings, a demonstration of the affection *Picasso* felt for Barcelona, the museum was extended to the neighbouring, *Palau del Baró de Castellet*.

It is an obligatory visit as day by day the number of visitors grows. It is the most complete and significant collection of the artistic works of *Picasso*.

Palau de la Música Catalana, by the architect Domenech i Montaner.

Palau de Berenguer de Aguilar, in Montcada
street, home of the Picasso museum.

At the end of *Montcada* street we find a valuable and beautiful example of Gothic art, the church *Basílica de Santa María del Mar*. Sumptuous and delicate, the main facade features numerous concentric archivolts. It was built between 1329 and 1383. Attention should be drawn to the high vault of the temple, supported by remarkably few columns separated from each other by 13 metres.

Continuing from Via Laietana to the Plaza Antonio Lopez, we find, sections of the *Roman walls*.

Once in this square we can see the building of *Correus y Telegrafs or Palau de Telecomunicacions*, in front of the remodelled port of Barcelona and the *Moll de la Fusta*.

Between this square and *Plaça Palau* we find the *Casa Llotja del Mar*, built between 1380 and 1390, at the height of Barcelona's maritime trade. The Gothic style, *Sala de Contratacions de la Borsa*, probably the

oldest in the Peninsula, is still conserved. The building houses the *Cámara de Comerç i Navegació de Barcelona*, one of the most important economic institutions in the country.

THE CITY OF GAUDI.

We now begin a very special chapter in the history of Barcelona, that dedicated to the work of the architectural genius, *Antoni Gaudí*, and which we begin in the so called "*manzana de la discordia*", in *Passeig de Gracia* between *Consell de Cent* street and *Aragó* street.

In this short space of *Passeig de Gracia* we find the different styles of the most important architects of Modernist art which completely predominated in Catalonia at the end of the last century and the beginnning of this present one.

Gothic Basilica of Santa Maria del Mar.

Of this architectural "discordi" the first example is the house of *Lleó Morera*, number 35 by *Domenech i Montaner*, who gave free rein to his preference for ornamentation. Number 39 is a *house in Luis XVI style*, by *Enric Sagnier*, but treated with discretion in its modernistic style. Number 41 is *Amatller house*, by *Puig i Cadafalch*, an expert in restyling the elements of northern Gothic and Renaissance Catalan. The next house number 43, *Batlló house*, work of *Gaudí* where he expresses his personal interpretation of Modernism, with the cult of the curved line. It is worth noting that *Gaudí* used the form of human bones for the configuration of the masses, balconies and columns of this house. A little further on in the same *Passeig de Gracia* at the corner of *Provença* street we find another priceless work of *Gaudí*. *Milà house*, better known as the "*Pedrera*" which was begun in 1905. It is said that when *Gaudí* was asked to justify the curvilinear volumnes of this construction he replied "*They are explained by their connection with the forms of the mountains surrounding Barcelona, visible from the site of the house*" On the other hand, it has also been said that in his conception of this mass of stone, *Gaudí* wished to portray the undulation of waves.

We must recognize that *Gaudí*, carried away with his intrepid inspiration, managed, with the "*Pedrera*", to suggest a superior destiny of transcendental aspiration rather than a house with flats and shops to rent.

Not far away, between *Provença, Mallorca, Sardenya* and *Marina* streets we find the most imposing of Gaudí's works, the *Temple de la Sagrada Familia*. Work on the construction of this church was begun in 1882, by the architects *Martorell* and *De Villar*. It was not until 1891 that *Gaudí* took over the direction of this project, destined to be the great Cathedral of Barcelona. His death, he was knocked down by a tram on 7th June 1926, prevented him. Even though he could not finish the work, at least his task was continued. When he took over the work, he modified his predecesors' project. He finished the crypt changing its structure for one with a more ambitious and original architectural structuring. In 1893 the apse was finished, still with signs of Gothic influence. Immediately afterwards the construction of the completely original *Nativity facade* was begun. He planned it in 1891, but during the construction it was changed in accordance with his constant desire to modify his artistic conceptions. By 1925, one of the four spires which now crowns this facade had been added. The other three had only been begun when Gaudí died in 1926, they were finished later, exactly as he had planned them.

The four towers above the facade of the Nativity.

The Nativity entrance.

Facade of the Nativity.

The facade of the Passió, finished by Subirachs.

The new artistic forms of Subirachs on the Passió entrance,
in evident contrast with the Gaudinian lines.

View of the towers and the Nativitat entrance from inside the temple.

The Sagrada Familia, aerial view. Rose window of the Nativity towers
Model of the project. Nativity entrance. Night view.

Casa Batlló. A terrace with the original touch of Gaudí.

With the *Sagrada Familia Gaudí* made an authentic demonstration of his artistic conceptions, at the same time showing a masterly technique, with absolute confidence in his own ability to defy the problems of disequilibrium and disharmony. This is Gaudí's greatest work and its continuation may respect Gaudi's original project. The church will have five naves without butresses, with an apse aisle of hexagonal radial chapels, covered by ellipsoidal vaulting supported on sloping columns. All the plans of the building are complicated hyperboloids. There will be three enormous entrances: the Eastern one, dedicated to

the *Nativity*, the Western one , dedicated to the *Passion and Death* of our Lord, and the Southern facade will be that of the Glory and *Resurection*, the biggest of all. Each entrance will have four spires, like the two already finished. A total of twelve spires will represent the twelve apostles. Four taller spires around the dome will symbolise the four evangelists. These four will surround an even higher one, 170 metres, representing the Saviour. It should be mentioned that at present the work of *Gaudí*, who is buried in the *crypt of the Sagrada Familia*, is being carried on by the Catalan artist *Subirachs*, who has finished the *Wes-*

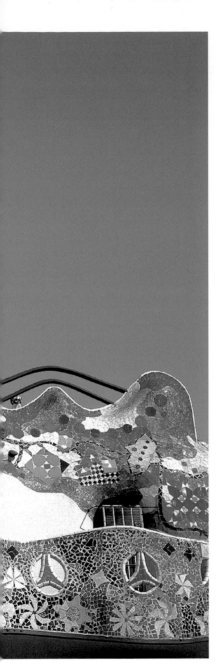

Casa Batlló, the dome of the facade on Passeig de Gracia.

Casa Batlló. Night view and reflexion of a building in Passeig de Gracia.

tern facade, breaking with Gaudí's style in a rather radical way, printing a new style on the facade of the *Passion and Death*, almost diametrically opposed to the Gaudinian conception, but standing out in the general framework of the *Sagrada Familia* and responding to the particular style of this Catalan artist, questioned, not so much for his modern artistic style as for its application in the church of *Gaudí*. His work is however, admired and seduces for its clean lines, the detailed cut of the figures, as well as the perfect harmony of the volumes without excessive pathos in the scene represented, which is, at this moment the normal entrance to the church.

We now go to the high part of the city, the *Salut district*, at the end of *Travesera de Dalt*, to visit the *Parque Güell*. It is the result of of donation made to the city by *Comte Güell* in 1900, with the express condition that *Gaudí* should take charge of urbanising the 15 hectares of land as and how he thought fit.

If the projected residential colony came to nothing, at least Barcelona could count with these gardens, unique in the world.

Window of Casa Batlló, where the oseous elements can be seen.

"Casa Batlló". Main facade
seen from "Passeig de Gracia".

Three aspects of Casa Milà, better know as "La Pedrera", also in Passeig de Gracia.

A detail of "La Pedrera's" roof.

The balconies of La Pedrera, simulating waves.

In 1912 *Gaudí* added the monumental bench in the *"hipostila" hall*, called the "*Sala de las cien columnas*" even though there are only 86 of them, it borders the upper terrace, intended to be the amphitheatre of a Greek theatre. It is something which, while starting off with painting, sculpture and architecture, cannot be contained within the normal limits of any of them. Besides the constantly curved forms, of the bench bordering the upper square of the park, it is composed of fragments of *Manises ceramic*, in different colours and sizes, arranged in the form of an enormous collage. The great variety of colours, the unforseen placing and combination has provoked great admiration, not only from the visitors and admirers, but also among great art critics. *Le Corbusier* wrote "*Gaudí is the man who has had most architectural creative force among all the men of his generation*".

In the centre of *Parc Güell* is the *Casa Museu Gaudí* where the famous architect lived until 1926, the year he died.

Gatehouse in Parc Güell in Gaudi's peculiar style.

Parc Güell. Wrought iron entrance gate.

The benches in Gran Plaça, finished in ceramic.

Windows of the gatehouse inside the park.

The Gran Plaça and the benches above
the "Sala de les cent columnes.

Ornate ceiling in the hipostila hall or "Cent columnes".

This house contains several objects which belonged to the artist, such as, paintings, personal objects, mementos and furniture by the same *Gaudí*.

Other works no less representative of Gaudí's genius are scattered throughout the city. In chronological order we mention first, *Vicens house*, in *Carolinas street*, built between 1878 and 1880, when *Gaudí* was 26 years old.

The Colegio de Santa Teresa de Jesús, in *Ganduxer street*, built in 1889, is a demonstration of just how much can be done with red bricks and parabolic arches.

The *Finca Güell* in *Pedralbes*, where the artist introduced a Moorish influence. The wrought iron entrance gate is outstanding, representing an original dragon.

Calvet house, built between 1898 and 1899 in *Caspe street*, a personal and free interpretation of Baroque style and his ornamental preferences with wrought iron.

Final we must mention *Figueras house* in *Bellesguard street*, better known as "*Bellesguard*" another, personal interpretation of *Gaudí*, this time in Gothic style. Besides the solid cross, crowning a daringly slender spire, the interior is well worth study. *Gaudí* built it between 1900 and 1902 on the ruins of the summer residence used by *King Martí*.

MONTJUIC, THE MAGIC MOUNTAIN.

One of the most attractive parts of the city is *Monjuïc mountain*. Which blends together art, culture, sport and history.

Montjuïc today is far removed from the Iberian city of *Laya* which was situated here; also lost in the mists of time is the temple the Romans built here to their God, *Jupiter*. Some historians claim that this is the origen of the name of the mountain: *Mons Jovis, Monte de Jupiter, Montjuïc*. Other historians say that nearer to our times there was a Jewish cemetery which gave the mountain its name, others state that the name was due to the great fame and influence in the city life of a Hebrew family called *Mont Judaic*.

Nowadays we must agree that great esteem the people of Barcelona have for *Montjuïc*, reached its

The dragon on the steps which lead to the Gran Plaça.

The buildings of the park with original pinacles.

Several aspects of the park. Above right, the learning columns in stone.

Below the Museu Gaudí, where the architect lived until his death in 1926.

A singular fountain, on the steps which lead to the Gran Plaça.

Curious details in ceramic, on the Benches in the Gran Plaça.

The covered walks in the park, in stone with leaning columns.

Dome of finca Güell and Col.legi de les Teressianes.

Wrought iron in finca Güell.

Casa Figueres, better know as Bellesguard, built on the ruins of King Marti's summer residence.

Arch by Gaudí in Manuel Girona street.

Casa Vicens, in Rambla del Prat.

View from the gardens of Mirador del Alcalde, on Montjuïc.

Costa i Llobera cactus gardens.

maximum with the celebration of the *1992 Olympic Games* which converted the mountain into a centre of worldwide attraction, and permited the realization of a dream.

The mountain can be reached from several directions. One of these is from the *Plaça d' Espanya*, in the *Gran Via de Les Corts Catalanes* at the beginning of *Passeig de Maria Cristina* which leads to *Montjuïc* by the *Font Màgica*. In the *Plaça de Espanya* there is a central fountain called *Font Monumental*, work of the architect *Jujol* and decorated with sculptures by *Osle*. The fountain has three sides which represent

the three seas which bathe the Iberic Peninsula: the *Mediterranean*, the *Atlantic* and the *Cantabric*.

Another way to get there is by *Miramar*, which we can reach from three directions: the costa de *Miramar*, the *aerial cable ca*r or the *Funicular*.

However,with present day *Monjuïc* we must begin by mentioning the great historical and archiological value of the *Castell*, donated by the Army to the city and, once restored to its original state, converted into *Museu Historic Militar*. The museum contains an unusual variety of valuable collections of all kinds.

Also worthy of looking at are the gardens of this

Montjuïc castle.

mountain, such as: *Miramar, Laribal, La Rosaleda* and *Font del Gat*, or those of *Mosen Cinto Verdaguer*, a monographic of exhibition of *bulbs, cactus* and other plants. The gardens *Costa and Llobera, Joan Maragall* and those of the 1929 Exhibition, designed by the *Frenchman Forestier*, which frame the now large area of the industrial fair.

A large number of exhibitions are held in this area every year, which has made Barcelona very popular from this point of view. This area covers approximately 15,000 square metres with several "palaces". One of them, the *Palau de les Nacions* has a hall with a capacity for 1,500 congress members.

One of the beautiful buildings on Montjuïc is the *Palacete* (little palace) *Albeniz*, which is the residence of the Spanish Royal family on their visits to Barcelona. It was a project of *Ros de Ramis, Ignacio Serra-*

goday and *Antonio Lozoya*. Inside are arts works by *Nonell, Casas, Rusiñol, Martí Alsina, Baixeras, Bayreda, Munoz de Pablos* and *Dalí*

One of the greatest works on Montjuïc is the *Palau-Nacional*, at the top of *Passeig de Maria Cristina* behind the *Font Màgica*. There is a large hall in the centre of this palace with a capacity for 4,000 people seated and an upper amphitheatre for several hundred more. It also contains one of the largest organs in Europe which has 11,000 pipes, 154 combinations, and 6 manual keyboards, plus one foot operated one. The *Museu d' Art de Catalunya* is housed here, the main part being the collections of Romanic and Gothic art. These collections are the most important in the world and, are indeed unique for the beautiful examples of IX to XIII century art. The frescos, murals, retables and carvings are priceless, the frescos

Palau Nacional and Font Màgica, from Passeig de Maria Cristina.

from *Sant Climent de Taüll* are especially splendid, with a *Panto-creator*, the *Virgen* and *the apostles*, all from the *XII century*. They were moved, using a special technique, from their original sites, where the bad climatic conditions and old constructions threatened these priceless works of art.

LA FONT MAGICA

In front of the *Palau Naciona*l and at the top of *Maria Cristina avenue* we find the illuminated fountain, la *Font Màgica*. A masterpiece of engineering applied to every possible combination of water and light.

View of the Font Màgica from Plaça d'Espanya.

The work of *Carlos Buigas*, the central basin is 1.8m deep, oval in shape, 65m long and 50m wide. It contains two smaller basins the lower one 35. diameter and the upper 12m. The rate of flow is 2,430 litres per second and the central jet can reach a height of 50 metres. There are twenty-nine different combinations of water which, together with the different lighting effects gives an almost infinite range of variations. The water is illuminated by 4,730 lamps with ten-colour filters . The fountain is directed by remote control from a cabin overlooking it.

At night one of the most beautiful sights is the magical aspect offered by *Passeig de Maria Cristina*, marked by small fountains in different shapes and colours,

framing, at the end, the *Font Màgica*, siluetted against the impressive background of the *Palau Naciona*l.

EL POBLE ESPANYOL.

The *Poble Espanyol* is a great tourist attraction, it was the project of the artists *Xavier Nogues, Miguel Utrillo* and *Ramon Raventos*. Built in 1927 for the 1929 World Exhibition, it is a unique project which groups the different architectural styles of all Spain, together in a special area.

The village is entered through *San Vicents* gate in the wall of *Avila which* surrounds the whole. In front is the *Plaza Castellana*, to the right are buildings in the

Various aspects of the Font Màgica, with its infinite variations of water, light and colour.

style of Caceres and opposite, through the *Pórticos de Sanguesa*, the *Plaça Major*, made up of buildings in the style of *Aragón, Burgos, Navarra, Catalonia, Soria, Castilla* etc., presided over by the *Valderobres* Town Hall. At the back on the left, the steps of *Santiago* surround a group of *Galician houses*. *Caballeros street*, evoking Castillian villages, leads off from the other side of this square, and from the *Arco de Maya, Pincipe de Viana street* recalls *Navarran Basque* architecture. In the *Aragonese Square* there is the bell-tower of *Utebo*, and then the *Adalusian and Catalonian districts* begin, with the streets of los *Arcos, las Bulas* and *la Davallada, Mercaders* and the *Plaça of the Prades Fountain* respectively.

Plaza Mayor in
Poble Espanyo
In the backgro
the Town hall
Valderrobles.

Caballeros Stre
in the backgro
the arch of Ma

Gradas de Santiago.

The gate in the wall which faces the sea is the *Portal de Bove*, *Montblanc style*. *Valencia* and *Murcia* are also represented around *Levante street*. Outside the walls there is a Romanic Monastery and church in the style of the *Catalonian Pyrenees*.

The *Plaça Major* is used for all kinds of popular festivities and demonstrations and there are several establishments where visitors can see arts and crafts practised.

The numerous bars, copying the taverns from other parts of the Peninsula and the pubs and discoteques, give the *Poble Espanyol* a festive air, much appreciated by the people of Barcelona, who go there to enjoy themselves in their free time.

L' ANELLA OLYMPICA

In reality the transformation of Barcelona, motivated by the Olympic Games, began with the demolition of the *Estadi de Monjuïc*, 17th October, 1986, to build the Olympic Stadium in the same place, conserving the old facade.

The new stadium retained the old *Marathon Gate* and the bronze horses, by the sculptor *Pau Gargallo*,

San Vicente Gateway, in the walls of Ávila.

Detail of the "Gradas de Santiago" and "Torre de Utebo".

Bulas street and "Torre de Utebo".

Caballeros street view from "Arco Maya".

Arcos street, in the
purest andaluz style.

above the stand. After remodelling this became a perfect installation for the athletes from all over the world who visited Barcelona to compete in the *XXV Olympiad*.

Following a long period of delicate and efficient work on this stadium, a mixture of antique and modern, the 45,000 spectators who filled the seats, could see, on

25th July, 1992, the two hour long *Inaugural Ceremony*, seen at the same time by millions of television spectators all over the world . The athletes and different artists such as the opera singers: *Montserrat Caballe, Placido Domingo, Alfredo Kraus, Josep Carreras,* and *Jaume Aragall* participated in this cere-

The National Art Museum of Catalonia (MNAC)

Original Pantocreator and frescos from Sant Climent de Taüll chapel, moved to The National Art Museum of Catalonia.

Palacete Albéniz.

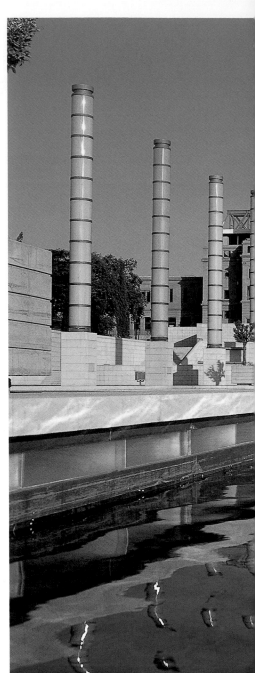

Several aspects of the Olympic Stadium. Below left, a moment of the 1992 Olympic Games opening ceremony.

mony. The honour of lighting the Olympic flame was given to the paraolympic athlete, archer *Angel Rebollo*, who sent an arrow straight to the centre of the bowl of an enormous torch fixed to the walls of the *Marathon Gate*. This flame presided over Barcelona'92 for sixteen days.

Doubtlessly this was one of the installations and events which symbolized the magic month of August 1992, but other sports installations also grew on *Montjuïc*.

Just in front of the stadium is one of the most beau-

tiful sports giants ever built, the *Palau Sant Jordi*, who many consider to be a architectonic jewel of Barcelona '92. It is the work of the Japonese engineer *Arata Isozaki*, who using modern technology and materials, created a space for 17.000 specatators.

The majestic dome is held up without columns or pillars, and was lifted at one time using a complex robotic system. The gymnastic competitions were held here. At the moment, due to its perfectly equiped halls and space, it is used for a variety of sports and commercial activities.

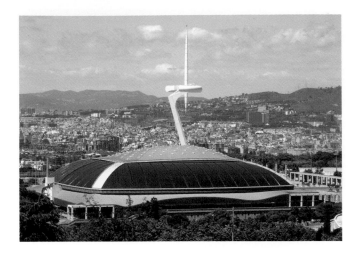

Several aspect of Palau Sant Jordi.

Palau Sant Jordi and Calatrava tower.

Interior Palau Sant Jordi

Opening ceremony of the Barcelona Olympic Games.

A little to the South of these two installations known as *Anella Olímpica*, we find a classic style building by the architect *Ricard Bofill*, famous worldwide for having designed, among other things, Les Halles of Paris. Designed to be *Universitat de l' Esport*, its monumental structure contrasts with the ultramodern design of the *Palau Sant Jordi*.

Beside this building we find the swimming pools, *Bernat Picornell* and a *baseball diamond* which, together with the two other installations described above, complete the buildings which surround the modern

Caixa Forum

Plaça d'Europa which connects them all. It is a modern avenue lit by two rows of street lamps in the form of columns and ending in a waterfall which springs from the Stadium.

In this same *Plaça de Europa* we find a unique communications tower. Built for the Games to establish an important communications network for these events. Its functional aspect did not impede the telecommunications engineer *Calatrava* from producing such a unique design that it has meant that the *Torre de Calatrava* will remain and not be demolished after the Games as was the original idea.

Other installations on *Montjuïc* which were improved for the Games were *Piscina del Poble Sec* and the old *Palau d'Esports*. A substantial revision of the whole mountain was also made, with the reconstruction of the gardens, look out points, parking and service areas as well as the *funicular* which connects the underground to the Miramar area. An escalator from *Plaça del Univers*, next to the *Font Màgica* and up to the *Olympic Stadium* solved the problem of mass access to the mountain which as was anticipated, has finally achieved the function the people of Barcelona wished for.

The *Museu Etnologic* and *Colonial*, the *Museu*

Torre Calatrava from Plaça d'Europa.

Monument to the Sardana. Below, Ethnologic Museum.

Joan Miró Foundation.

Arqueologic, the *Mercat de Les Flors*, the *Teatre Grec* and above all the modern building of Miramar which houses the *Fundació Miró* are also worthy of mention. The Fundació Miró is an enormous, complex building, for exhibitions, where a synthesis of the work throughout the life of the Barcelona artist is displayed. His particular style has left its mark on various points of the city. The building was constructed by *Josep Lluis Sert* and was officially opened in 1976, as the *Fundacio Joan Miró i Centre d'Estudis d'Art Contemporani*.

In the upper part of Montjuïc park, in front of the *Mirador del Alcalde*, beautiful gardens with a view of the Barcelona Port, we find the monument to the *Sardana*, work of the sculptor *Jose Canas*. It represents a dance scene typical in Catalonia and, in some way captures the idosyncrasy of the Catalan people. It is a homage to this dance of which is said, *"it is the most beautiful of all the dances which are made and unmade"*, a moto representative of this dance of a group with joined hands.

In front of the monument to the Sardana further up the mountain we find the telecabin which connects

Teatre Grec.

Monumental font in Plaça d'Espanya, dedicated to the three seas.

Night view of Montjuïc mountain.

Animation in Passeig Maria Cristina
during the Olympic Games.

Miramar to the Montjuïc castle, which in turn connects
with the *aerial cable car*, which crosses Barcelona
port, from Barceloneta to Miramar.

MUSEUMS AND CITY ART.

Besides the stamp Gaudí left on Barcelona, other
artists have also been important to this city whether
for their Catalan origin or for their love of the magnificent atmosphere of the exhibitions of art to be found
in Barcelona. This can be seen in different museums,
statues and buildings scattered throughout the city.

This is the case of the previously mentioned *Picasso Museum* in *Montcada stree*t, which occupies the

Entrance to Picasso Museum.

Picasso Museum,
hall dedicated to Las Meninas.

Berenguer de Aguilar and *Baró de Castellet* palaces.

In principle the donation of Jaume Sabartés was the basis for the creation of this museum but the contribution, by the Town Hall of a large number of Picasso's works, previously kept in the *Museu d'Art Modern de Barcelona*, was important to the opening of the Museum. This was later enlarged creating a example of the works of Picasso unique in the world.

The different halls where the paintings are exhibited together with the historic value of the building, are an authentic artistic jewel for the city. Among the works exhibited we find *El Arlequin*, the oil painting *Science and The ill child*, this last belonging to the *"blue period"* of which there are several paintings in the Museum.

Another visit no less interesting is to the *Fundació Joan Miró, Centre d'Estudis d'Art Contemporani*. On Montjuïc mountain, near Miramar. When opened this foundation exhibited a collection of Miró's drawings from the period between 1901 and 1975. Later in 1978 this museum was recognised world over as a *"fundacion ejemplar"* by the *European Council*. Some of Miró's most beautiful works can be seen here. The work of this artist can be seen in other parts of the city too, for example in the *Prat airport*, where there is a large *mural by Miró*.

One of his most peculiar works can be seen in the Plaça del Escorxador. A monolith called "La dona i l'o-cell" which deals with a symbiosis of harmonic and colourful symbols, using tiles by *Llorens-Artigas*.

The beautiful interior of Palau de Berenguer de Aguilar.

Interior Picasso Museum.

"La Dona i l'Ocell" by Joan Miró, in Plaça de l'Escorxador or Joan Miró.

Mural by Miró in
Barcelona airport.

"La Cadira" by Antoni Tàpies, on
top of the Tàpies foundation.

Several aspects of
Serra house or "Puntxes"
by Puig i Cadafalch.

Joan Miró, who was born in Barcelona in 1883, exhibited for the first time in 1918 and afterwards moved to Paris, where he first connected with the *cubist movement*. He soon left this tendency to develop his own particular style, nearer to *surrealism*, but without a doubt his own style, both for the lines and colouring found in his works.

Continuing with the contribution *Miró* made to "street" art we have the *mosaic* in the *Plà de la Boqueria* in *Les Rambles*.

Another Catalan artist, *Antoni Tapies*, whose work is always controversial, corresponds to the surrealist artists who still paint. We can see his work in a foundation very much in style with his work. The *Fundació Tapies* is in *Aragó street*, between *Rambla de Catalunya* and *Passeig de Gracia*. On top is a strange

L'Hospital de Sant Pau, of Domenech i Montaner.

Dome of La Rotonda, obra de Adolf Puig i Casamitjana.

Lleó Morera house in "La Manzana de la discordia".

wirey sculpure called by the artist, "*La cadira*" (the chair), but a good imagination is necessary to discover where this chair is.

At the foot of Tibidabo we find the *Museu de la Ciencia*, dedicated to science and its progress. It is a living Museum where there are continual innovating exhibitions in the field of engineering and technique. Contrary to the other art museums, in this one it is "*forbidden not to touch*", as the exhibitions are eminentally functional and the visitor is expected to activate the inventions and experiment with the new formulas of movement, energy, etc.

Other artistic demonstrations in Barcelona are the buildings. The growth of "*Modernism*" found fertile ground in this city and if *Gaudí* concluded the most original modernist works, Barcelona is full of buildings, public but above all private, of great archtectonic value. Among those to be mentioned is the House of "*les Puntxes*" in Diagonal avenue, work of the architect *Puig i Cadafalch* and in general the diverse works left by *Francesc Berenguer, Lluis Domenech i Montaner, Joan Rubio i Bellver* and other architects, thanks to whom, Barcelona aquires a different air to other cities in the Peninsula.

Ametller house, by Puig i Cadafalch.

Arnús house
on the skirts of
Tibidabo, by
Enric Sagnier.

Palau de la Música.

Comalat house
by Salvadó Valerí
i Pupurull.

The Casa de *"Les Puntxes" by Puig Cadafalch*, in *Diagonal* on the corner of *Roselló street*, was built at the beginning the century and combines, in good taste, the original restyling of Gothic with the Modernistic tendencies of the time.

Not far away, in the same *Diagonal*, next to *Passeig de Gracia*, we find another original building, the *Palau Robert*, a magnicent example of urban architecture. It is in a rather *French style*, built between 1901-1902 by the architect *Joan Martorell*.

The Cascada Monumental, in Ciutadella Parc, by Josep Fontserré and Antoni Gaudí.

THE CIUTADELLA.

Another point where we can find many artistic demonstrations is the park, *La Cuitadella*. The demolition of the old fortress, built in the old Ribera district after the War of Succession, made it possible to convert this space into a beautiful area of museums, gardens and a zoological park for the Universal Exhibition in 1888. The work of the architect *Josep Vilaseca*, this park has three principal avenues called respectively, "*de los alamos*" (poplars), "*de los olmos*" (elms), and "*de los tilos*" (limes). A large lake gives the beauty and distinction water always confers on gardens. The most spectacular monument is the *Casca-*

Ciutadella lake.

Martorell Museum and
Museu d'Historia Natural,
by Domenech i Montaner.

Parlament of Calaluny
in Ciutadella Parc.

Desconsol by
Josep Llimona.

The Zoo. "Copito de Nieve".

da Monumental, not far from the lake. In Neoclassical style it is the work of *Josep Fontsere* and *Antonio Gaudí*. The statues are by *Venanci Vallmitjans* and the *Cuadriga de la Aurora* right at the top in bronze, is by *Rosend Nobàs*. On the other side of the lake is the pla-za de Armas. Surrounded by an attractive garden and a pond, in the centre of this square, is the nude statue "*Desconsol*" by *Josep Llimona*. Opposite we find the *Parlament de Catalunya*, in a building constructed in 1748 and the old Arsenal de la Ciudadela, now conver-ted into the *Museu d'Art Modern*, where we can admire paintings by *Fortuny, Rusiñol, Casas, Nonell, Zuloaga* and *Solana* and sculptures by *Llimona, Clarà, Gargallo, Viladomat, Clarassó, Huguet, Rebull, Miró, Tapies* and Salvador *Dalí*. Among the many works of art distribu-ted throughout the gardens, it is worth mentioning the mounted statue of *General Prim*, the monument to the *Voluntaris Catalans de la Guerra 1914-1918*, by *Josep Clarà* and the *Dama del Paraguas* sculpted in 1888 by *Roig y Soler*, which has since become an amusing and romantic symbol of the city of Barcelona.

Animals of all kinds and varieties can be seen in the

L'Arc de Triomf, by Josep Vilaseca and freize by Llimona.

zoo which contains more than one hundred and sixty installations, including lawns, patios, ponds, cages etc. in which the different animals are housed. There is also an important *Aquarium* where the trained dolphins, seals and whales perform for the pleasure of the spectators who go to see them.

At the entrance to the Zoo we can see a monument dedicated to *Walt Disney*, by *Nuria Tortras*. A homage to the cartoonist whose popular animals became celebrated personalities in his films. Before leaving the park we can visit the *Museu Martorell*, dedicated to petrography and the *Museu d'Historia*

Natural, the work of *Domenech i Montaner*.

Leaving the park by the *Passeig Lluis Companys*, we can see the monument to *Ruis i Taulet*, Mayor of Barcelona and promotor of the 1888 Exhibition. On the right we find the *Palau de Justicia*, finished in 1901 to the plans of *Sagnier, Domenech* and *Estapé*. Inside there is a hall of "*pasos perdidos*" with paintings by *Josep Maria Sert*.

At the end of Passeig Lluis Companys, is the *Arc de Triomf*, which was the main entrance to the 1888 Exhibition. It was designed and built by *Josep Vilaseca* and has a high frieze sculpted by *Llimona*.

Aerial view of Tibidabo. In the foreground the Templo del Sagrat Cor de Jesús.

TIBIDABO AND COLLSEROLA HILL RANGE.

The final part of this book is dedicated to the most interesting areas away from the urban centre, such as *Tibidabo*, in the *Collserola Hill Range*, where on the highest point we find the up-to-date attraction park with all kinds of installations, a natural observation point over the city and a *Museu d'Automates of Tibidabo*.

It can be reached by car up the winding *L'Arrbasada* road or that of *Vallvidrera*, or by the *funicular* which connects with the old *Tramvia Blau* which starts from *Avinguda del Tibidabo*.

Right on the summit of the mountain we find the *Temple Expiatori del Sagrat Cor de Jesús*, work of the architect *Enric Sagnier*. The crypt is open for use and above that is the Temple. It is built in Gothic style but not without a certain majestic grandeur.

From inside one can reach a high platform with a magnificent panoramic view. A bronze statue of the

Night view of the Templo Expiatorio by Enric Sagnier.

Panoramic view of Barcelona from Templo Expiatorio del Tibidabo.

Fabra observatori. The city in the background.

Several aspects of the fair ground.

An impressive view of Barcelona from Tibidabo. In the foreground, the giant big wheel in the fair ground.

Sagrat Cor stands on the highest spire of the temple.

Near the summit is the *Observatori Fabra y Gabinet de Fisica Experimental Mentor Alsina*. This observatory was donated to the city by the marqués de *Alella*, *Camil Fabra* in 1904.

A little lower down is the *Torre de Collserola*, work of the English engineer *Norman Foster*. This communications tower is the highest building in the Peninsula, more than 200 metres high and its daring design is visible from any point in the city. The tower has a viewing platform open to the public.

On the skirts of Collserola, already in Barcelona is the mountain *Sant Pere Martir* where we find *Cuitat Universitaria*, with different faculty buildings, *Political Science and Economics, Advanced Mercantile Studies School, Higher School of Architecture, Saint*

The Typical Blue Tram: Tibidabo Avenue.

Collserola tower by the engineer Norman Foster.

A beautiful
night view
of Collserola
Tower.

Pedralbes district,
on the skirts of
Collserola.

Entrance to the Gothic precinct of Monestir de Pedralbes.

The Gothic purity of Monestir de Pedralbes,
which houses the Thyssen art collection.

The modern building of
the European University
in Via Augusta.

Entrance to Barcelona by Diagonal Avenue.

The faculty os History, Barcelona University.

Two views of Footbal Club Barcelona's stadium "Camp Nou".

The Barça Museum, whith the European Cup won in 1992.

George's Fine Arts School, School of Industrial Engineers, Science Faculty, Faculty of Pharmacy, Faculty of Medicine, Faculty of Law, and Faculty of History. The Law Faculty is outstanding among these with its Great Hall and murals by *Jaume Cuxart*, equipped for all kinds of Congresses.

Near these faculties we find the *Camps d'Esports Universitaris*, the *Reial Club de Polo*, the *Club de Tenis Turó* and the installations of *Barcelona Football Club* with its magnificent stadium, the *Camp Nou*, with a capacity for one hundred thousand spectators.

This stadium is one of the finest sports constructions in the world and a visit to it and its *Museu del Barça* is a "must" for all who visit Barcelona and wish to understand what this club means, not only to Barcelona but to all of Catalonia. Work on the Camp Nou was begun in March 1954 and was finished three years later. It was inaugurated on 24th September,

1957, day of the Mercé, patron saint of Barcelona, to whom the members of this club dedicate their trophies. The initial building, later added to, was the work of the architects *Francesc Mitjans Miró* and *Josep Soteras Mauri*, to the orders of, the then President *Miró Sans*.

In the Trophies room in the *Museu del Barça*, we can find the cups corresponding to the different competitions won by this club in its long and protracted history, not only in Football, but also in different sections such as Basketball, Handball, Hockey on skates, Ice Hockey, athletics, Baseball, and Artistic ice skating.

However, there is no doubt that its most appreciated trophy is the *European Cup*, won in 1992, for the first time in the history of the club.

The *Palau Blaugrana*, the *Palau de Gel*, the *Mini Estadi* football ground, and others which surround it make up the whole of F.C. Barcelona's installations.

Palau Reial or Pedralbes.

Near here we find the *Palau Reial* or *Pedralbes*, built between 1919 and 1925 by the architects *Borrás* and *Nebot*. It contains valuable works of art and is richly decorated.

In this same area of the city we find the *Reial Monastir de Pedrables*, an invaluable part of the rich architectonic collection of old Barcelona. It is in the upper part of the *Pedrables district* and was founded by *Queen Elisenda de Montcada*, wife of *Jaume II*. It was planned by *Guillem d'Abiell* and its builders

Ferrer Peiró and *Domenech de Granyena*. It was begun in 1324 and finished in 1412. Among the notable speculcres in the Monastery, the most outstanding is that of the Queen-founder, with its prone statue sculpted in alabaster. At present part of this monastery houses the valuable *Thysen* art collection.

In this same district we find the *Club de Tenis Barcelona*, one of the best installations for this sport to be found in Europe

Reial Club de Tenis Barcelona.

María Cristina Square.

PARC DE MAR AND VILA OLÍMPICA.

On the other side of the city, in the *Gran Vía de les Corts Catalanes* and *Passeig de Carlos I*, is the *Plaza de Toros Monumental*, with a capacity for 19.600 spectators.

Starting from the bullring, *Plaza de Toros Monumental*, in the direction towards the sea, we find Barcelona's latest urban development, called Area de *Parc de Mar*, it has meant the definitive opening of Barcelona to this Mediterranean, which has washed

Plaza de Toros Monumental.

The speed circuit and new olympic area in Vall d'Hebron.

Passeig de Lluís Companys and Arc de Triomf.

Mistos (Matches) by Claes Oldenburg.

The modern building in Parc de Mar.

its beaches from the beginnings of time. The old *Poblenou* district, seat of industrial Barcelona in the XIX century, was the scene of one of the greatest works for the Olympic Games. The railway lines were buried, the *Estació de França* remodelled, and the old *Estació del Nord* converted for sports events and exhibition hall.

Barcelona's sewage system was amplified and the construction of a residential area with 2,000 flats, office blocks and a hotel with more than 20 floors was planned.

From this the *Vila Olympica* was born. The best architects in the country worked on the plans. In front of this completely new district, called *Nova Icaria*, there are seven kilometres of new beaches and a sports harbour. It is becoming an important residental and leisure centre. Its wide avenues and gardens, innumerable terraces and restaurants in front of the sea make it one of the areas of Barcelona with more futurure. It connects with the *Passeig Maritim*, also finished in 1992 and with the *Barceloneta beaches*.

Another new area created for the Olympic Games is in the *Vall d'Hebron*. Five hundred flats, a tennis club, two multisports installations and the connection

New forms around the Vila Olímpica.

BAR Tower

FORUM

Bogatell Beach.

The new Passeig Maritim and retreived Barceloneta beaches.

between the two new districts, the *Cinturó del Litoral* and its continuation, the *Ronda de Dalt* have given this city a definite push towards the year 2000, with the hope that the new century will bring as much hope and prosperity as the previous XX.

The last part of this book is dedicated to the Barceloneta and the Barcelona's beaches, in homage to the opening up to the sea produced by this latest urban transformation.

Barceloneta is a fishing district and was intended to house those who lost their homes when the old *La Ribera* district disappeared. It was begun in 1753, to a project by *Próspero Vervoon*, with one storey houses. However, in 1837, the *barón de Meer* authorized the addition of another storey to each building and it was the general *marqués de la Mina* who authorized construction of this popular Barcelona district, which was the first "*eixample*" of Barcelona.

Barceloneta Beach.

The ols fishing port, Port Vell, maaintains the classic air of Mediterranean fishing ports.

The definitive "*Eixample*" was carried out to the plans of the engineer *Ildefons Cerdá*, regular blocks of flats 100m by 100m, in straight streets, which have an invariable width of 20m, and right angle cross roads, *Passeig de Gracia, la Rambla de Cataluyna* and la *Diagonal* were the only exceptions. Now with the latest constructions on the coast, the clearing of the *Barceloneta beaches*, finishing the *Passeig Maritim*, at the end of which the *Port Olimpic* was built and the creation of seven new beaches in the *Poblenou* district, this part of the coast has undergone one of the most beautiful transformations which could be given to Barcelona. The dream of a city, eminently seafaring and portuary, open to the sea, definitely its great destination which had not been fulfilled until now.

Of all the different ways you can arrive in Barcelona, railway, road, plane or ship we prefer this last. To leave as well, to see the image of the city siluetted at the foot of Tibidabo mountain slowly fade away. This was how the first visitors, invaders or conquerers, saw it. It is the best image we can keep of this old seafaring city, cosmopolitan and commercial. Its streets full of art, history in its walls and vitality in its people. This is how we should like you to remember it.